Forex Trading

Forex Trading 1 and Investing for Beginners 2

By Sam Sutton and Stephen Smith

Trading Forex

*The Basics You Need to Immediately
Make Money from the Forex Market*

Sam Sutton

Table of Contents

Investing for Beginners

Introduction

I want to thank you and congratulate you for downloading Forex: The Basics You Need to Immediately Make Money from the Forex Market.

I've always had a passing interest in economics. From keeping up with the latest blogs to listening to my favorite economics podcasts, economics has been intriguing to me for years. For years I also heard about the various markets of exchange where traders could make money. Bonds, stocks, options and Forex were a staple of the programs that I listened to and the blogs that I read. After hearing so much about the Forex market, I had a sudden thought that brought me to start investing, who exactly invests in the Forex market? It was in discovering the answer to this question that I realized you don't need to be a trained or seasoned investor to get started in Forex; you just need to have the will to learn and the discipline to execute trades with patience.

Over the last two years I have gone from having a causal interest in Forex markets to gaining over half of my income this year through Forex trading. My foray into Forex was not without its challenges, but with the knowledge that I have gained, I want to make investing and profiting in Forex as simple a transition as possible for you. I will teach you the key pieces of information that you need to know so that you can start trading right away. Whether you want to take an analytical approach or a news and policy approach to trading, I will teach you everything you need to know so you can get started right away.

If you decide to approach Forex but miss the essential lessons I offer then you will be starting in Forex at a huge disadvantage. Forex trading is more than just making a few good calls – it's about understanding the mechanics of trading and knowing when to pull back trades or when to increase your total investment. Trading is a marathon, not a race; I want you to be successful in Forex trading not just in the immediate, but also for long into the future. Without the knowledge that leads to consistency in profits, Forex is little more than an attempt at legalized gambling. You can take the gambling approach, but I know that with just a few lessons you will be in a place where you can find success in the long run.

It's time to make a change in your life; it's time to get invested in Forex. There are opportunities to make money at any time of day from your home, but these opportunities are hidden behind knowledge of skills and an understanding of the markets. This is what I offer, the skills to make intelligent trades that will allow for long term success in Forex trading. Continue reading and soon you will know all of the necessary information to grant financial freedom for yourself and your family.

Did you know that a large percent of people who make a lot of money lose it within the first couple years?

It doesn't take much for a person to lose all of their money. Around 2 in 3 lottery winners lose all of their winnings within 5 years. If someone could lose hundreds of millions of dollars over a couple years, how fast will you lose your millions that you could make from this book?

Over the past couple years I have stumbled upon the key secret behind managing money and KEEPING it. If you follow the link below you will uncover the truth behind managing and keeping the money you make

>>> Click/Tap here to Learn the Secret Behind Money Management <<<

Sam Sutton

Chapter 1: The Basics of the Forex Market

Faith, Currency and Gold

If anyone discovers that I have a love for economics, I usually get a cold or confused response. The reaction all comes form the sentiment that economics could not possibly be interesting, but I believe this is merely because economics is often framed incorrectly. So much of modern economics is thought to be extremely mathematical, and while this is certainly true, economics wasn't always this way. At one point it was more about the study of how humans that don't know each other interact. It is the study of relationships that form around a center of money. I start with this concept because as you begin to trade in Forex, it's important to understand both how the Forex market works and how we came to rely on this system. Understanding these fundamentals have helped me grasp the interplay between countries and has improved my trading overall.

The global Forex markets as we know them today are very different from how currency prices were determined just fifty years ago. You know that Forex markets control the pricing of different currency, but before the currency system countries relied on a gold backed system. There are some that would claim a gold backed system is better than what our economy currently uses, and while there are some merits to this system, our current global economy is far better at handling financial crisis due to a key change in the monetary system of most large economies. The gold system was merely adopted first because of the rarity of gold, and because it is inherently an easy system to understand.

For a moment, consider a piece of currency that you have on you. Whether that note is a twenty dollar bill, or merely a quarter in your pocket, ask yourself; what gives this coin or bill value? It's a simple question but one that is actually quite complicated in the abstract. Before the current financial system the value of your dollar was merely a placeholder for gold that the United States held. The gold of the United States was essentially disturbed around the country through the form of their minted currency. The economy of a country was therefore highly dependent on that nation's supply of gold. If you think back to your history classes in high school and middle school, you may realize that much conflict over the last millennia had roots in obtaining more gold from foreign powers or new land that had not been claimed. This system is simplistic in how it works – it's fairly simple to realize that the currency in hand supplements gold, but it also makes for a lot of difficulty in terms of currency conversion.

For centuries the best way to convert currency was not to go through a government institution, but rather to go through large banks that issued their *own* currency. This currency was a note that allowed traders to use their hard earned money across multiple nations. The banks that ran this system profited immensely, as they were providing a much necessary service that government institutions were simply not handling as well.

The question about what gives your money value is simple in terms of the gold standard, but we can see problems in terms of generating real wealth on a level of nations, and also that exchanging currency was highly problematic, often requiring third parties to handle currency exchange through their own intermediary currency. Today's system is far better, but the answer to the question of valuing currency has changed greatly. In simplest terms, the currency that you have on your persons is valuable simply because you think it is valuable. There is no gold backing your dollar bill; it cannot be exchange in value of any precious metal (dollars used to be exchangeable for gold). The value of the dollar is a collective agreement across the world economy that the dollar is worth something. Understanding this premise that currencies today are largely based on a faith based system, you can start to see how modern currency exchange works.

There's a reason I asked about the value of the US dollar specifically; it is the currency that all other world currencies are traded in. Meaning that if you want to buy Euros or Chinese Yuan, you will be making a transfer in US dollars. From this initial transfer, we have the Forex markets starting to take shape. As currency is traded back and forth, the respective volume and demand of currency is what shapes their value, along with the interaction of various national banks and institutions that can change the money supply. For example, the US dollar's value is based on three inputs: one, that the dollar inherently has value as a tradable item and is recognized across the world. Two, the dollar's value is based on its trading volume and how in demand it is relative to other world currencies. Three, the Federal Reserve has the authority to print money, and this will reduce the value of individual dollars through inflation. Through these three inputs, partially based on faith, the rules of supply and demand and the whim of a government body, we have our modern Forex system.

For your part, you will be making money off of the fluctuations in currency. We'll be getting into the specifics of how currencies are traded, but to give you a simple idea of how you will make money, let's work with a simple example. Suppose that you were to go on a trip to Europe – anywhere in the Euro-zone that accepts the Euro. Before your trip to Europe, you decide to exchange some spending money so that you go shopping and go out to eat. This transaction is an example of a currency pair, in this case the USD/EUR currency pair. If you decide to exchange 500 dollars to Euros, you would currently get 463.59 Euros. The rate of transfer here was 0.93, meaning that for every 1 USD you were provided 0.93 Euros. On the way back to the United States, you realize that you made all of your purchases through your bank card, and that the total amount of 463.59 Euros are still in your possession. You decide to exchange this money back for US currency on your way back to the United States. The transfer of 0.93 has changed, and is now 0.91, meaning for every US dollar you receive 0.91 Euros in return. In this case, the USD has decreased in value relative to the strength of the Euro. When you make your exchange back you are left with 509.44 USD. That's right; in this trip you managed to make ten dollars simply through the fluctuation in the currency rate.

This simple demonstration shows a lot of the specific ways in which foreign exchange currency works. You always purchase currency as a pair, so you are trading on the strength of one foreign currency versus another. Currency pairs are standardized, as is this one: USD/EUR. As the ratio increases, the value of the USD goes up and the Euro goes down. As the ratio decreases, the Euro gains in strength and the USD depreciates. This small-scale example is exactly how Forex works – you make a bet on a currency, hold that currency for some period of time as the price exchange changes, and then sell that currency when you are able to make profit. There are many ways of determining the ideal currency pairs to buy into, but regardless of the strategy, the method to profit is always the same.

The Value of Forex Traders

Forex message boards are a great place to reach out to other traders and learn information about the markets. It can be difficult to find the most useful information on these boards, and some questions certainly come up more often than others. One of the most common topics on these message boards pertains to the value that traders grant to Forex. When you think about what the role of a Forex trader is, it is hard to come away with the idea that they are anything other than speculators. This term, 'speculators' has a negative connotation to it, and I wanted to clarify a bit where the value in the economy comes from with Forex trading.

I gave a simple example of how you can make a profit through Forex with the exchange of dollars for Euros and then back again. The change in the conversation rate was precipitated by the supply and demand of each currency on the Forex market; meaning traders were responsible for the ten dollars of profit in this currency exchange. Why they happened to increase the value of the Euro versus the dollar is where the traders' real value comes in; they are setting the exchange rate for more than your trip, they are also determining the price of imports and exports in a country. In this example, it became cheaper for Europe to purchase items from the United States, specifically because their currency now grants them more USD per a single Euro. This change in their purchasing power allows for more output from the United States because their products are more competitive on a global scale. All of this is due to the work of currency speculators working in their own interests. By trying to determine the value of a currency in the future, all Forex traders work together to set the market rate for currency exchange, and in turn facilitate global trade by setting fair prices for exchange.

If the value that you offer by trading on Forex is still not clear, I want to leave you with one last thought, the power of markets. Imagine if it was the single responsibility of someone to determine the world's currency prices. This would be an immensely difficult job, as it would be up to a single person to determine values based on so many inputs that his or her job would be nearly impossible. When dealing with so much information that could influence the price of a currency, you need thousand of people working in coordination and sifting through all of the different factors that could determine currency prices. The point is that the work of the collective that individually is working in their own self interests, provides a better value for currency prices than any government body or single entity working to regulate the market. The value of the individual trader is that they are added to this collective of information that is determining the value of the currencies across the market.

Chapter 2: Requirements to Start Trading

Broker

You will need a broker to get started with currency trading. There are two schools of thought to how you should select a broker. You can either go with whomever has the lowest rates and a wide consortium of currency pairs to trade, or you can pay a little more to have access to research specific tools offered by particular brokerage houses. It is my strong suggestion for beginners that you merely go with the cheapest brokerage house. Even small firms will trade at least forty or fifty currency pairs, with the larger markets trading around ninety. This is not a function of the cost of the broker, but rather selecting one based on size and influence. Paying for advanced brokerage tools is the main driver in higher fees, but these tools will not be of us to the inexperienced trader. Also, it is dependent on a particular style of trading that you may not gravitate towards. Go with the cheapest broker, learn how to use their specific tools for analyzing currency pairs, and then move to a more expensive broker in a couple of years once you fully understand how analyzation tools should be used. This is a mistake that I've seen a lot of traders make, where they will use expensive tools but will not quite understand all of the measurements. In depth analytical approaches take years to master, and a long time to simply learn how to understand the resulting data. Early on, you will be using easier analytical strategies that won't require such computation.

In order of brokers that I would recommend, please refer to the following list. None of these brokers offer extensive research tools, but they have a wide variety of currency pairs and their rates are extremely moderate. Also, as you are starting out I understand that you might not have the largest investment pool, as such there are some brokers that have heavy minimums while others will have no minimums at all – this by itself might be the determining factor in choosing your broker.

Oanda   (No Minimum)

Ameritrade   ($2000 account minimum)

FOREX.com   ($250 account Minimum, only 50 currency pairs)

FXCM ($50 account Minimum, only 39 currency pairs)

ATC Brokers   ($5000 account Minimum, only 35 Currency pairs)

Capital Requirements

Making money through Forex markets is not a race; it is a marathon. To ensure that you have the right amount of capital and that each trade you make is not eating too far into your investment fund, we have one simple rule: the 10% rule. This rule will allow you to trade long into the future, by ensuring that no single investment is too large to maintain. As you are starting out, I suggest that you do not use any leverage, meaning that you do not buy any currency on credit. In addition, you should start trading with $1000, with a $3000 account really necessary to make any significant amount of money through trades. Remember that brokers' commissions will eat into your profits, so you will want to make trades between $50 and $100, at a minimum. Nothing is more disappointing than making a great trade but not making that much profit because your investment pool was not large enough.

If your investment fund is not on par with the sizes I described, then you will start to run into the temptation of spending more than 10% on a single trade. With the ten percent rule, you are encouraged to at *most* spend $100 on a $1000 account. If you are starting off with $250, even a $50 trade is more than twice what you should be comfortable with. The plan is that you are successful with about 70% of your trades. If you accept that 30% of all trades will either net you zero profit or possibly lead to some losses, then this ten percent rule starts to become really important. As you start to set up your investment fund, make sure that you can take on this risk and that you are prepared to only spend ten percent of your fund on any single transaction.

Understanding Your Investment Fund

There is a mistake that I see a lot of traders make – they do not create a salary for themselves based on their profits from Forex trading. This is a rather basic idea about savings, but your venture into Forex markets is similar to an independent job. Working alone, you are going to have to manage your investment fund as if you were the boss of your own company. It is important therefore that you separate your investment fund from all of your other finances. Your investment fund should be considered for one thing, Forex trading and nothing else. You cannot draw from this fund to pay rent, buy food or even consider it your retirement account. It must be fully separate from all other savings accounts, including emergency accounts and college funds.

The second aspect of your investment fund is that you should always be working to increase the size of this fund, not because you want to use that money immediately, but so that you can increase the maximum size of your trades. As your investment fund increases, so does the maximum that you can trade according to the ten percent rule. Your goal then for making true profit and holding onto that profit should come from a salary that you pay yourself based on your investment fund. Over the last two years I have seen my investment fund grow much larger, and in that time I have paid myself roughly 20% of the total growth of the fund. 80% of the profit that I make from trading goes right back into the investment fund, allowing for continual growth in my profits. I believe that you must think about your investment fund this way, and that you must separate it from your paid out profits and any other funds that your household may have.

Understanding the Time Commitment

Depending on the strategy that you use to approach Forex markets, Forex may take up a few hours of your week, or it could take a few dozen hours. The two basic strategies rely on either a value trader or a day trader mindset. The main difference between these two is the time commitment to trading. A day trader needs block hours to commit to trading, so think about trading for six to eight hours in a single session.

A value trader makes a trade and holds onto it for several days, weeks or months, meaning that they just have to do the initial research up front, and then can monitor their investments every week. As you start trading, you are likely to do a mix of both. Unlike day trading in other markets, Forex offers the unique ability to be traded at any time of day. There will always be currency markets that are open to trades, regardless of where on the planet you call home. You may need to trade late at night to get those block hours for trading, but this is one of the fastest ways to profitability.

Within two or three months, you will have a sense of the type of trading that leads to the most profit, and then you will have a much better sense of the average weekly time commitment. In short, plan for around ten to twenty hours a week to start, and as time goes on and you find the strategy that works best, expect this number to either go up or down. I know many traders that now work on Forex full time, so if your profits come in at a nice rate, this may also be an option for you, allowing for enough time in the week to focus on day trading or research for value trades.

Chapter 3: The Mechanics of Trading

Knowledgebase

Like any industry, there are industry specific terms to Forex that are essential to start trading. These are just terms that the industry uses for common measurements and to facilitate faster trading. Make sure that you know what each of the following terms are and where they fit into the larger picture of trading on Forex – this is the essential knowledgebase you will need to start trading.

Pips

A Pip, or pips is how traders refer to movement in Forex holdings. One pip is a movement in the ten thousandth decimal place, or .0001. If the currency pair USD/EUR moves from 0.93 to 0.9350, it is said to have moved fifty pips. A pip is not a complicated concept, but rather is emblematic of how currency pairs shift in price. They move in very small increments and this is the most significant decimal place that is worth noting. Currencies fluctuate at smaller rates than a pip, and at times several thousand greater than a pip, but the pip is the most basic measurement that we have when it comes to an individual currency pair.

When looking at currency pairs, you will see changes measured in pips. In addition to just a handy metric, you can also use this to demine your profitability minus broker fees. For example say the USD/EUR is trading at 1.1, and then has an increase of 27 pips, or changes to 1.1027. In this case the US Dollar increased in value. If you wanted to determine your total profit in this move of 27 pips, you use a simple calculation: First multiply your total investment by the conversion for pips. If you invested $1,000 USD in the US currency, this is expressed as $1000 * .0001 = 1$. Take this number and divide it by the currency trading rate of the currency pair: $1/1.1027 = .91$. Now we take this number, representing the dollar per pip ratio of profit and multiply it by the number of pips .91 * 27 = 24.57. From this investment and a fluctuation of 27 pips, you have made $24.57, minus fees.

One additional note, while the pip generally refers to the fourth decimal place for all currencies, there is an exception with Asian currencies, where a pip is merely the second decimal place. For example one pip in regards to the Japanese Yen is reflected as 0.01. This is merely because of the way that the relative value of these currencies is stated. These currencies do not use decimal places, but rather have multiplied everything by one hundred to come up with relative prices. As such, think about 100 Yen as 1 USD; it makes sense pips are moved over two decimal places. Keep this in mind in regards to these Asian currencies, as it can be misleading unless you understand how pips are measured in these markets.

Stop-Loss Orders

Stop loss orders are a very helpful tool for traders, and even when not invoking the specific tool available from your broker, it is helpful to at least set up mental stop-losses for yourself. A stop-loss order is a lower bound for when you wish to pull out of a trade. You can issue to your broker an order saying that if a currency pair reaches a certain price, then you should sell all of your holdings. Stop-loss orders are exactly what they sound like, to stop you from losing any more money in the market. These orders are particularly helpful for value traders that are not monitoring their holdings constantly, and also for day traders that are working with many different currency pairs and have many different investments simultaneously.

Even when you don't set up an actual stop-loss order with your broker, you should set up a mental stop-loss. Find a price point where you no longer feel comfortable staying invested. Early on, this was a saving grace on trades that were not going well, but also when I wasn't sure if I wanted to stay committed. A huge part of being a successful trader is overcoming fear and staying true to your convictions. When real money is on the line, it is hard to determine the time in which you should pull out. A stop-loss order removes a lot of this stress because you are making a decision when your money is not at stake, allowing you to think through the risk in a reasonable way. The way in which I like to determine by maximum losses is percentage based. For example, if I make a $100 investment, the most I want to lose is twenty percent. I either have a mental stop loss order if I am monitoring the investment and it is a day trade, or I put in a physical stop-loss order with the broker if it is a value, or long term trade. Knowing your limits and using this feature from your broker will be essential in your early days and months of trading.

Currency Pairs

In chapter one you saw how money could be made from the exchange of currency and the passage of time. Specifically, you saw the transfer of US dollars to Euros and then back again. This is an example of a currency pair. When you buy into a currency, you are always buying into a specific currency pair. The base in which you pay for a pair is always in US dollars; so don't worry about where to get some of the first currency in a pair to buy the later, as US dollars are all that you will ever need. Currency pairs show a dynamic relationship between two countries, where the currency pair is reflective of the purchasing power of one country over another. In chapter one with the example of the Euro, European nations gained purchasing power over United States goods because of the decline in the US dollar's value. This is merely one example of how this dynamic relationship is useful to investors and businesses outside of strictly Forex markets.

Currency pairs are thought of as either standard pairs or exotic pairs, where exotic pairs fluctuate at a greater rate and/or have a relatively small volume. Exotic currency pairs are riskier to trade because with a smaller pool of investors, you lack the type of clarity in information that comes from trading larger currency pairs. Also, the small volume means that you may have difficulty offloading a currency at the time at that you want to. The reasons for the volume and volatility changes in exotic currency pairs are largely a function of one or both of the countries in a currency pair. The smaller the economy, the more volatile the currency is due to outside influence of the world – also the lower number of traders makes each trade more significant in changing the value. Examples of exotic currency pairs are: USD/DNK and USD/NOK. That is, the US dollar pegged against the Danish Kroner and Norwegian Kroner. While you may not think about Norway or Denmark as volatile countries, remember that is not what defines the exotic pair. Keep this in mind as you look at currency pairs, as it is not always obvious what is a standard pair versus exotic, although some brokers will actually label currency pairs as such.

Spread

If you are buying USD on a Forex market, you are not buying that currency directly from the US government. It is not being created out of thin air, but rather you are buying it from another trader. Understanding this, it makes sense that the trading value of a currency is rarely the actual value that you will obtain that currency for. The trading value is merely indicative of the average of the last few trades, or in some instances, the most recent trade. The people that you are buying currency from are traders like yourself, and they will want to make as much money as possible. To help buyers and sellers meet, we have the spread, which is the difference between the *ask* and *bid* price of a currency. For example, suppose that a currency pair is trading for 1.21, meaning you would gain 1.21 * the base currency's value in an exchange. You may only be able to find this currency trading at 1.2099, or a little higher or lower demanding on the demand. If the price that you are willing to pay is 1.21, but the best the seller can offer is 1.2099, we call the difference between these two numbers the spread. In this case, the spread is 0.001, or ten pips.

The reason why you need to keep the spread in mind is because it is a useful indictor for telling the direction that a currency is heading in. As the spread widens, it becomes more difficult to buy or sell a currency pair, as the spread narrows, the currency is highly liquid. An increase in spread usually means that a reversal is due, or at a minimum the currency value is going to slow down. You will want to use the spread to predict for future values, and also to gain insight for the best possible time to sell a currency. For standard currency pairs, volume will not be an issue, but for more exotic pairs the spread really starts to affect your ability to offload your holdings. How much the spread will be an influence on your ability to trade is therefore going to depend on the currency pairs that you are trading. As a beginner trader, you are best off starting with more established currency pairs so that you do not have to worry about volatility.

Candlestick

The candlestick is one of the most essential graphs for looking at the price history of a currency pair. A candlestick is a type of line graph that shows the fluctuation of price, where Y measures the price and X measures the time. What's unique is how each data point is represented:

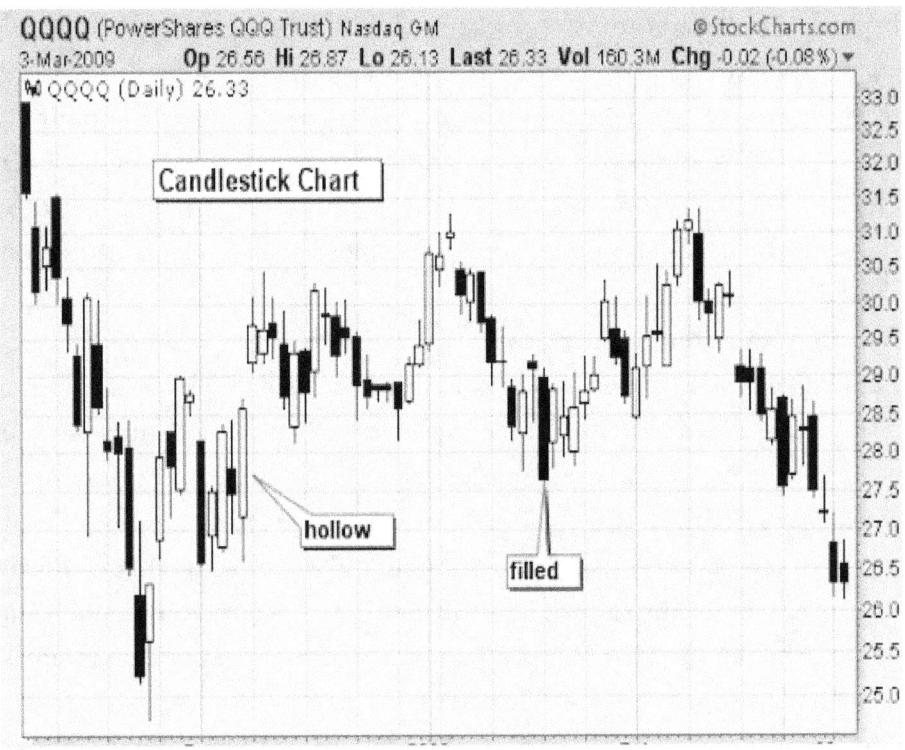

The above graph may seem quite confusing at first, but what is on display is a tremendous amount of information in the simplest way possible. Here we can see the simple X axis as time and the Y axis as price. The data points are made of candlesticks, where the filled in blocks represent declines in price, and the white hollow blocks represent an increase in price. This is at the heart of how candlesticks work, where by seeing this bit of information on each data point, you can see how each data point stands relative to all past data points. You can see that it is an increase or decrease at the flash of an eye, allowing you to measure a currency pair in different time intervals to different effect. Put simply, this graph could be presented on a yearly basis, daily basis, or over the last hour, where each data point could represent the month, day, hour, minute, etc. The candlesticks themselves are the individual unit of time in which we are measuring a currency pair. In addition to the candlesticks themselves, you will see a bar extruding from the top and bottom of the bar. This shows the magnitude of the change, where a tall bar at the top shows a positive change and a bar at the bottom shows a negative change. As for the length of the body of the bar, this shows the volatility in the currency's price, with longer blocks showing more volatility. If you invoke primarily analytical strategies this will be one of your main metrics, as you will thrive on volatility.

Reading a Currency Pair Graph

Remember that a currency pair is defined as a single ratio. As you are just getting started it can sometimes be difficult to identify how a currency pair ratio will affect the currency pair as a whole. For example, working with the NZD/USD pair, or New Zealand Dollar/US dollar pair, we can see the current exchange rate is 0.73. Imagine that you own US dollars and want to make a profit, in this scenario you would want this number to decrease. Looking at a graph this would be measured as a line with a negative slope. Please engrain in your head that as a line is going upwards, it is good if you are holding the first of a currency pair, if the lien is going downwards it is good if you are holding the second currency pair. I know this is a simple concept, but trust me when I say that a lot of people tend to read these graphs incorrectly. They are so accustomed to only wanting to see growth and a line chart go up, that they sometimes forget that is not in their best interest. I've seen this happen to smart people before – it is just a facet of this single ratio not always being intuitive for finding the positive direction for a single currency.

Options on Currencies

Don't trade options on currencies – this should be reserved for more advanced traders. That being said, some useful information can be gleamed from options markets for currencies. Very briefly, I want to explain the two types of options and what they mean. We have call options and put options, and each is the inverse of the other. With a call option, you are betting that a currency value will increase. With a put option, you are betting a currency value with decrease. If you see in the options market for currencies that there are a lot of calls on a currency, it means that a number of options traders believe that currency will increase in value. If you see a lot of put options, it is a signal that traders believe a currency value will drop.

Lastly, the way in which these options work is that they give the buyer of the option the choice to buy or sell currency for a certain price at a later date. In a call option, I'm betting a currency value will go up, so I pay a price for a contract that allows me to buy a currency pair for a lower price if the currency pair hits a certain price by a certain date. For example, if I am invested in the USD/EUR pair, and want the US Dollar to go up in value, then I pay for a contract that says I can buy USD at *today's* price if USD is trading at X by a certain date. If that date passes and USD has not reached that value, then the contract is worthless. If the price is met, then I can buy USD for a cheap price and sell it right away. Put options work in the opposite direction, where if I wanted USD to go down in value, I would pay for a contract that says USD will hit X price by a certain date. If USD goes down to that pre-arranged price then I can buy USD for a price set in the contract and then sell it right away. The contract will specify that I can buy it at a lower than currency market value, ensuring that I make money right away.

I wanted to give you a quick explanation of options because they are helpful for analyzing the market, but also to note where options traders make their money. Many options traders simply *sell* options, and they only make money when a contract does not go into effect. Keep this in mind, as this should be a powerful deterrent to starting with options. Traders early on will buy options based on the contract price, not realizing that even though the contract was well priced, the odds of the contract going into effect are astronomically low. Avoid options, but pay attention to what a number of call or put options on a particular currency pair mean.

Price Action

Price action is merely a term used to refer to how well or poorly a currency pair is trading. You can think about the price action as the 'swings' of a currency, whether that is positive or negative. In general, it merely describes a trending price movement in a currency pair.

Market Hours

One of the great things about Forex trading is that you will be able to trade day or night. There are markets that are open at all hours of the day. Look at the following list and you will see what exchanges are open and when. All the times listed are in standard Eastern Time, so adjust for your own time zone. Do note also that exchanges will sometimes sell the same currency pairs, and some exchanges will specifically sell other currency pairs. Also, the volume on these exchanges is not always the same from country to country. The New York exchange has greater volume than Sydney, for example.

New York: 8AM-5PM EST

Tokyo: 7PM-4AM EST

Sydney: 5PM – 2AM EST

London   3AM – 12PM EST

Chapter 4: Analytical Approach to Forex

Premise

I have two main methods of approaching Forex markets. I have found success in both strategies, but as you are just starting out and wrapping your head around the basics of the market, I suggest that you start with an analytical approach. What this means is that you are making trades purely based on existing trading data. You don't need to be tapped into the world of global politics, nor do you need to be aware of trade deals and agreements between companies across the world. You are merely looking at specific indictors and trading based on this data. This is a great trading method for beginners, and at upper tiers is great for statisticians or those that are apt at manipulating data. The best way to improve your analytical trading skills is to get better at using the various metrics for determining what currencies will rise, and which will fall.

Day Trading

Day trading is my primary strategy when it comes to Forex. This has been my bread and butter for two years, and although I have branched out in recent months, day trading has proven to be the main driver of my profits regardless of the climate in the markets. The premise to day trading is that you are holding onto currencies for a very short period of time, and are using cyclical data to predict ideal entry and exit points for a currency.

My typical day with this strategy starts by waking up two hours prior to whatever market I'm trading on. For example, I live on the east coast and typically trade on the New York exchange. I get up at six and start looking at currency pairs by around 6:30. I use the time before the market opens to identify currency pairs that have cyclical volatility, or rather have moved the last few days but have typically evened out by the end of the trading day. This is quite common to see in Forex markets, and there will be a general cycle to currencies, and in the long run they may lose or gain a few pips, but from a day-to-day approach they lose and gain value several times throughout the day. It is going to be through these small movements in a single trading day where I am going to make my money.

Once I have identified somewhere between three and five of these currency pairs, I plan my exit and entry points. You know that volume matters in terms of being able to sell off your holdings – if I am trading on exotic currency pairs that I pay strict attention to the volume of trading throughout the day, otherwise I can merely find the best price point to enter. When trading low volume currencies, you will need to pay closer attention to the spread to ensure that you are buying in and cashing out at the right times. Let's work with two quick examples.

In example one, I am going to buy a common currency pair, GBP/USD, or British Pound and the US dollar. I have decided to buy this currency pair because the price has been on a rotation for a few days, tending to hit max trading price at noon and going down again before the close of market. I decide that the time to buy is right as the market opens, because this is likely the time when it will be at the lowest price. I have also noticed that the stock is on a cycle of around 30 pips, meaning it moves about thirty pips each day. I decide that I will try and sell my holdings after around 30 pips of movement, and collect the profit for that day. This is a fairly straightforward example, and is the type of currency trading that you should focus on as you are just getting started. The type of tools needed to research this currency pair are fairly minimal, and looking at candlestick graphs for the last few days of trading would show this rotation in the currency pair's value. I have the leisure of waiting for around 30 pips of movement because this is a commonly held currency – I don't have to worry about my ability to offload my holdings. I would want to pay attention to the spreads to cash out when they are most in my favor, which in this case means narrow spreads.

For another trading example, let's work with a more exotic currency pair, USD/DNK. This is the US dollar trading against the Danish Kroner. In this example I am focusing on gaining value through this currency pair in a single trading day. The primary difference is going to be when I start to position myself for exiting the market. Suppose that this currency pair is trading at a cycle of 30-37 pips everyday for the last three days. I can therefore estimate that this currency pair will move this number of pips on the day that I take my position. I buy into this currency pair, hoping that the value of the Kroner will go up 30+ pips. Finding my entry point was a matter of finding the average lows for the last few days, assuming that the currency would not fall below that low on the day I take my position. Now here is the tricky part; we need to pay close attention t the spread for exotic currencies to be able to cash out at the ideal time. I'm expecting movement of 30 to 37 pips, but I'm actually going to start selling my holdings around 27-29 pips. Am I cutting into my potential profits? Absolutely, but it has happened to other traders and myself many times that if you wait for maximum profit on exotic currencies, the trading volume is so low that you end up cutting into your profits. Wait until over 3o pips and you are at tremendous risk. First of all, the price may not change by another 7 pips; it may start to decline at 30. Remember that this movement is merely an estimate, so we are looking at the lower bound and assuming this is when the price will hit its peak. As long as we start selling before the peak, we will make the most profit.

In short, day trading is a preferred style for many early Forex traders. The advantages are that research can be done outside of market hours (looking for the next day), and the tools that you need are not too advanced to be able to determine good picks for this strategy. If you start with two to four picks with a day trading strategy, you want to find success in around six to seven out of every ten trades. You are going to make very little profit on some of these trades, but this is where you will find improvement. It's simply a matter of being able to more accurately read graphs, but with day trading a standard candlestick for 24-72 hours, or even a line graph will be sufficient to find decent picks in the beginning.

Swing Trading

Swing trading has a lot of the same ideas as day trading, but the time scale is expanded to a few days instead of a single trading day. Fundamentally the strategy is the same as day trading. The main difference comes in how you use research tools to estimate the movement of a currency pair. There are two main techniques that I use to find currency pairs that are good for swing trading. Personally, I find this to be a little more research intensive than day trading.

The first technique is to focus on the immediate trading history of a currency pair. If you can find a currency pair with high volatility for one day, look into their past the last few days and see if you can start to identify a pattern. These cycles are not going to be as consistent in day trading, so the stretch from high to low is going to be more random. What you are looking for is merely the impression of a cycle; and build the parameters based on what you find. For example, suppose that you are interested in a relatively stable currency pair: GBP/USD, or British Pound to US Dollar. You see that there has been a lot of recent volatility and you start to look back a few days. You notice that yesterday, the pair moved -15 pips. The day before yesterday, the currency moved +10 pips. Three days ago the currency moved +12 pips. Four, five and six days ago the movement was: +7, -15 and -10, respectively. We may have found a good currency pair to get invested, but contrary to day trading, we want to buy our currency pair towards the end of the day, or when there is the least volatility. We may have a cycle of the currency moving for a few days in one direction, and then shifting in a second direction. We can use another tool to help us identify if this is a cycle, or some other occurrence maybe related to politics or volatility in the news. Checking the movement of the currency against the 25 day and 300 day high and lows for the currency

28

pair, we can see that the currency pair is within its highs and lows for these two time periods. What this means is that it is increasingly likely that you have identified a cycle. Since the trading highs and lows are not outside of normal bounds, the pair is currently within well known territory, so we know that this is totally normal and expected behavior. Since the currency is not hitting new highs and lows, we can assume that within our cycle, we have a lower and higher bound for the cycle. We will want to buy in at the 25 day low, and then hold the currency until it has moved around 45 pips – this is based on the trading data for how far swings move for this pair.

The second technique is the functional opposite of the first. At first we were looking for currency pairs and making sure that their cycle is within the 25 and 300 day trading highs and lows. In the second technique we want to find currency pairs that are trading outside of either their 25 or 300 day highs or lows. It doesn't matter if they are trading above or below, just that they are different. In the first case, you find a currency pair trading below its 25 day high and low. From this, look past at the last few months to see how often it has climbed back from its lows. If it has consistently climbed back, buy into this currency pair. You will also want to look at the relationship of these countries and see if there is any recent news that is causing the price change in the currency pair. If there has been a news event, I would not trade on this currency. It is no longer predicable. If there is a no news or political cause for this price shit, you should get invested because there is bound to be a rebound based on the history of that pair's pricing.

In the second case, a currency is trading above its 300 day high. This is very unusual indeed, and might even call for shorting the currency through options, however you should only go down this path if you've been trading for a few months. The first thing you should do is look at the relationship between these two countries and any news that might have warped this relationship. You will almost certainly find that something has changed – you don't have breaks from 300 day highs or lows without some sort of event causing a shift in a currency pair's pricing. Based on this event, and the implications, you can start to buy in or short a currency pair. In this second case, it is very difficult to determine the amount of time that you should hold onto a currency. We are almost out of the realm of cycles, however we used analytical tools to find our position in this currency pair. We just confirmed or denied the relationship based on the news media from both countries. In the next chapter you will find that this is similar to a type of value trading, with the main difference how we came to find our picks. We based it on a change in the value of a currency based on the 300 day highs and lows, instead of jumping to the media to find a currency pair's relationship.

Scalping

Scalping is a top tier strategy. Like day and swing trading, you are still looking to identify cycles. The key here is that you are working on very, very small time intervals. I'm talking about buying a currency and holding it for less than an hour before selling it. This is a strategy that I strongly urge you do not focus on as you just start trading Forex. The key to developing a strong scalping method is to learn candlestick charts, and to gain insight into small cycles with your broker's toolset. For myself, I don't focus on scalping because the only way to make a really great profit is to take massive positions on a currency. For example, scalpers typically need to invest twenty to thirty thousand dollars to make a decent profit of a few hundred dollars. This simply isn't in the realm of many early traders. Even for myself I feel that the risk is not worth the reward in scalping. I merely wanted to include scalping in this section to inform you of this trading style, and also to look out for traders that have taken this approach to trading, as it will explain some of the rapid price movements or changes in spread – changes that cannot be explained with other trading strategies.

Chapter 5: Value Trader Approach to Forex

Premise

Value traders take a very different approach to currency trading. While I focus on day trading, an analytical approach, I find that value trading is a great way to make longer term currency picks. These tend to individually pay off greater than day trading, but I find that they are altogether harder to find, limiting your number of active trades. The mentality of a value trader is that they are trying to find for market inconsistencies for a traded currency. Imagine the Chinese Yuan and how it is matched to the dollar. Ignoring that the Chinese Yuan is a harder currency to trade in general due to the heavy regulation from the Chinese government, the Yuan has a different issue in that it is currency not pegged to the right rate. This is not a secret – any economist and a handful of politicians will make the same claim. Relative to the US dollar, the Chinese Yuan is much stronger than its current trading value. For a value trader, they would buy as much Chinese Yuan as possible, and wait for the currency conversion to dollars be more favorable before they cash out. Now you can't actually do this with the Chinese Yuan due to some restrictions in how the currency is traded, but it serves the example that value traders are looking for currencies that are not pegged to the same rate. Finding currency that are traded free and fairly but are not traded on the correct rate is much harder to find than the Chinese Yuan, a well known manipulated currency.

Global Interdependence

Taking a value trader approach to Forex means that you need to be keyed in on how countries interact with each other. There is a strong relationship to the dollar and the Mexican Peso. For example, I know that if a number of car manufactures were to open plants in Mexico, the currency would experience a minor change change in favor of the Peso. This change will take months, if not years to be reflected in the currency price. Acting on this news I buy a stake in the Peso and wait for the currency to change. At the same time though, there are other elements that determine the trading value. A wall between Mexico and United States, or a change to the way that NAFTA (North American Free Trade Agreement) works, and suddenly my long term position might seem like a foolish investment. This is the risk and mechanics of this style of trading. You are trading based on news and information and your understanding of how countries interact. Profit is made when you are accounting for enough factors that will determine the price in the future. Mistakes are made when traders do not account for the proper variables.

Basic Strategies

Value traders tend to work in longer time frames than analytical traders, meaning they simply hold onto a currency for a longer amount of time. You should note that as a value trader you do not need to hold onto a currency for a long while to make a profit. During the 2016 US election, I was exchanging dollars and Pesos at a fairly rapid rate, only holding onto either currency in the pair for a few days. I was trading based on recent news events made popular by Donald Trump. He would go onto the campaign trail and start criticizing Mexico, or claiming that our trade deal was quite poor. When this would happen, the Peso would fall and the dollar would rise accordingly. I could have purchased dollars in this currency pair and made decent profit, but what was amazing was that the Peso always bounced back after Trump made a statement about Mexico. It was during this bounce back of the Peso that I made my profits. Some of these jumps were large, in the hundreds of pips. The time scale for investment in this scenario was only between one and three weeks. This is the type of value trading approach that I would suggest just as you get started in Forex. You don't want to trade on the complex interplay of countries based on long term relationships because odds are you do not understand every facet of those relationships. Instead, try a different approach and work based on news events and the immediate fallout that occurs.

2017 and On

I never thought the 2016 election would have lasting ramifications on the Forex market, but here I stand in 2017 with Donald J. Trump as the president of the United States. Never before has the trading market been so ripe for value traders to benefit off of the great instability that Donald Trump brings to the global economy. I have been working on theories to define the relationship that Donald Trump is going to bring to the global economy, and what I have found is not too far off what I discovered about Mexico. As a general rule when Donald Trump interacts with a country that is friendly to the United States, historically friendly as in helping in World War II, that currency gets strong for around a week. At the time that this book is being written, Trump has already made numerous statements and criticized many different countries. Most recently was a phone call between the United States and Australia. The AUD went up compared to the dollar because of this negative fallout from this phone call.

Here's how I would make trades in the future based on Donald Trump. When the United States and another country interact positively, the dollar goes up. If they interact poorly, the dollar goes down. Any statements made that affirm Russia as a global superpower or put NATO in jeopardy, and the Euro falls relative to the dollar. These have been the simple connections that I have found that have worked for my trades. I will continue to buy into currencies based on the impact of Trump, and I suggest you do the same.

Conclusion

Thank you again for downloading Forex: The Basics You Need to Immediately Make Money from the Forex Market.

You now have the skills necessary to start trading Forex and making immediate profit. Your first step to start trading is to choose a broker based on the currency pairs that you want to trade, the best rates, and the size of your investment fund. Refer to chapter two for a list of my preferred brokers. Next you will want to start with the analytical method of day trading to benefit from Forex. Note that this method has the advantage of you closing your balance books at the end of each day. In your first month of trading, it is good to know how well you have been doing on a day-by-day basis — a reason for sticking to this method as you first start trading. Remember that you will also want to start with standard currency pairs as you are trading, and hold off on exotic currency pairs until you've noted good trading volumes in currency pairs that you are interested in.

As you start trading and gaining experience, you will become better versed in how to manipulate trading data using your broker's tool set. It will take you around three months to truly get in the groove of making good day trading calls with high consistently. After you've reached this point, I suggest that you start making some value trades. These are trades that you are going to hold onto for a longer amount of time, but you are making these decisions based on news and the current geopolitical climate. Note that chapter five has a basic summary of some of the currency changes that you can expect in the future. If you can think through the interplay of countries, like how changing NAFTA will affect the CAD/USD pair, or the USD/MXN pair, then you will be in a position to earn tremendous profit.

As this book comes to a close, I want to stress the importance of building up your investment fund and never breaking from the ten percent rule. Always focus on building up your investment fund as a way of making larger trades, and never risk more than ten percent of your total fund. You have the tools to start trading, you have the knowledge, but you lack the experience – stick to this rule and you will be trading long enough to reap the benefits of this rule and the increased investment pool it brings.

Lastly if you enjoyed this book, it would be much appreciated if you could leave a review on Amazon. The best way for this book to make its way into the hands of more readers is through truthful reviews about this work. Please write what you liked about this book and what could be improved upon. Any and all feedback is helpful as I continue to serve the needs of my readership.

Thank you and good luck!

Did you know that a large percent of people who make a lot of money lose it within the first couple years?

It doesn't take much for a person to lose all of their money. Around 2 in 3 lottery winners lose all of their winnings within 5 years. If someone could lose hundreds of millions of dollars over a couple years, how fast will you lose your millions that you could make from this book?
Over the past couple years I have stumbled upon the key secret behind managing money and KEEPING it. If you follow the link below you will uncover the truth behind managing and keeping the money you make

>>> Click/Tap here to Learn the Secret Behind Money Management
<<<

Description

Have you ever considered supplementing your income through trading on Forex markets? It's a thought a lot of young traders have, that they can enter the Forex market and walk away with profits after mastering the Forex trading 'game'. The truth is not so simple however; Forex trading requires skills and strategies for the average trader to be successful.

Most traders that enter the Forex market without the skills and the knowledgebase required will lose their investment money quite quickly. This is where I want to aid you in starting your venture into Forex. I aim to teach you everything you need to know about the market, where to get started and how to start making profits immediately.

Continue reading and you will find practical solutions and strategies to trading in Forex. I offer a guide to making money written for those that have not yet invested in Forex. With work, determination, and the information in this book, you will be trading currencies and making profits in no time.

In This Book You Will Find:
- Everything you need to know about Forex markets and how to start trading currencies.
- A fleshed out and developed guide designed for beginners, but written by an expert.
- Key approaches using analytical and value trading perspectives to drive profits in Forex markets.
- An explanation of the tools and metrics you will be using to make the best trades.

Investing for Beginners:

The Only Money Guide You'll Ever Need

Introduction

Congratulations, and thank you for purchasing *Investing for Beginners: The Only Money Guide You'll Ever Need*.

Once upon a time, getting into the world of investing was only possible if you were incredibly wealthy, or if you knew someone who could help you. Otherwise, investing was pretty much ignored by many. In fact, a great deal of the population actually feared the idea of investing, as they were concerned that they may lose all of their money.

The reality of investing has changed significantly in the past several years. Nowadays, people who don't invest are almost certainly doomed to have a poor relationship with money. Those who do not take the time to learn how they can effectively invest are essentially putting themselves directly at risk of inflation, which is an inevitable experience of our modern world.

Fortunately, you do not have to be incredibly wealthy or have a friend with the right know-how to get involved in investing. Instead, you simply need to have a sum of money to get started with, nearly any sum will do, and you must also have the desire to learn. Through this book, I am going to teach you the many ways that you can get started with investing and how you can begin to make your money work for you.

Throughout each chapter, you will learn to understand why investing is so important, how it can help you increase your income, the primary things that you need to know about investing, and which investment strategies are the best for you. By the end, you should be feeling confident in your ability to produce a wonderful investment portfolio that will serve you for years to come.

If you are ready to tap into a wonderful money-making opportunity that was once only reserved for the elite few, then this book is the perfect read for you. I hope that you are able to learn plenty from it and that by the end you feel confident in your ability to build your investments wisely, strategically, and successfully. Please, enjoy your read and be sure to follow the tips provided so you can get the most from this book!

Did you know that a large percent of people who make a lot of money lose it within the first couple years?

It doesn't take much for a person to lose all of their money. Around 2 in 3 lottery winners lose all of their winnings within 5 years. If someone could lose hundreds of millions of dollars over a couple years, how fast will you lose your millions that you could make from this book?

Over the past couple years I have stumbled upon the key secret behind managing money and KEEPING it. If you follow the link below you will uncover the truth behind managing and keeping the money you make

>>> Click/Tap here to Learn the Secret Behind Money Management <<<

Or Go to https://secretstomoneymanagement.gr8.com/

Chapter 1: Benefits of Investing

Investing has many wonderful benefits behind it. The primary benefit is that you will increase your savings so that you have more money in the long-term. However, this is not the only benefit that you will reap from investing! Let's explore what the many benefits of investing include.

Long-Term Returns

One of the biggest benefits of investing is that you increase your potential for long-term returns on your investments. For example, if you invest in a stock market and ride it out, in a few years' time the stock increases significantly, you then increase the amount of money you have. This is typically the biggest reason why people begin investing in the first place. The idea of being able to invest whatever amount you have available in something that will essentially sit there and increase the value of your funds over time is exciting. Knowing that your money is not simply sitting there and being stagnant, but rather it is actively growing on its own means that you can feel confident that you are taking active and effective measures toward your financial growth in the long run.

Don't Suffer From Inflation

One of the problems with simply keeping your funds in a savings account is that it does not rise with inflation. If you have your money sitting in a savings account, the purchasing power of your money significantly decreases over time. That is because you have the same amount of money, but the value of goods is always increasing. Essentially, this is no longer an effective way to hedge yourself against inflation and ensure that you have a healthy 'nest egg' anymore. At one time, savings accounts were powerful and people did not need to worry about purchasing power or inflation. However, that age has long since passed. Inflation is a very real risk and it regularly becomes an issue for virtually anyone who has not taken the time to invest.

If you invest your money effectively and properly, the value of your money increases as the value of commodities increase. This means that your money is inflating alongside the active market. As a result, you know that your purchasing power will remain strong. You will always know that the money you have set aside is plenty enough to cover the rising costs of goods. Rather than worrying that inflation will cripple you, you will know that you are actively and smartly working with the market alongside inflation, rather than slowly drowning beneath it.

Creating a Residual Income Source

Investing is a wonderful way to create a source of residual income. The profits you earn from your investments are gained through very minimal work on your behalf, depending on the types of investments you have chosen to make. Some of these may not be accessible for some time, though other forms of investments are accessible immediately. For example, if you invest in real estate. Not only is the property itself inflating in value over time, but you can also rent out the property and earn monthly income from the property.

Residual income is a wonderful way to boost your monthly and annual salaries to ensure that you will always remain in a financially strong position. In modern times, residual income truly is the best way to protect yourself and ensure that you always have plenty of money to use and invest at any given time. This means that should your linear income (money earned directly for your work or invested) ever be reduced, or even be taken away for some period of time, you still have some level of income available to you so that you can maintain your lifestyle.

Invest Based on Your Needs and Abilities

Investing in the modern world truly gives you a wide variety of options to invest in based on your needs, as well as your abilities. This means that investing has become something that is so simple virtually anyone can get involved with it. You no longer have to fit specific criteria so you can invest. Instead, you simply have to be ready to learn how and be willing to take the leap.

Regardless of where you are at, moneywise, investing allows you to consider what you want to gain from your investments and how you can gain that specifically. This means that you can easily choose what you desire: increased profits, protecting your purchasing power, residual income, etc. and then use that as your primary objective when investing. This means that you can gain virtually any financial benefit from your investment.

The fact that you can invest based on your unique abilities is also important. This means that no matter how much money you have per month or year to invest, you can still get started. Given the many different ways that investing can take place these days, there are no longer strict and large requirements in place before you can get started. The minimum buy-in value ranges, with many investment funds being made available at nominally low prices so that virtually anyone can become involved with investing.

Little to No Action Required

Depending on what you plan to invest in and how much of your time you want to invest in it, investing can take little to no required action to get your desired results. Instead, you can easily choose strategies that require absolutely no time at all. Or, alternatively, you can choose ones that require you to be involved and allow you to keep yourself directly in the line of action with your own investments.

Some examples of choices that allow you to refrain from becoming overly involved include investments made available to you through your bank, mutual funds, and cryptocurrencies. These are ones that can typically be left alone for quite some time. On the other hand, investments that can take more of your time, (unless you choose to hire a manager to overlook your investments) include stocks, real estate, and other commodities.

Prevent Temptation

If your money was already invested, this makes it significantly easier to prevent yourself from being tempted to use it. Many people see funds building in their savings accounts and have a tendency to encourage themselves to dip into it 'just this once.' This can become almost addicting, and before they even know it, they're right back where they started. This can be a major and frustrating cycle for many people. Putting a fair portion of that savings into investments where they can be held long-term makes it much easier for you to ensure that you don't give in to temptation and draw on your savings since they are already allocated and are more difficult for you to access.

As you can see, there are many benefits for people who want to get involved in investing! If you are ready to or are interested in reaping all of these wonderful rewards, you know that investing is for you. Truly, there are no downsides to investing. Nowadays, with how easy it is for people to become involved and the number of benefits that you stand to gain when you do, it is a no-brainer as to why you need to start investing as soon as possible.

Chapter 2: Choosing Your Investment Strategy

Now that you understand how important it is that you begin investing, and the many benefits you stand to gain as a result, you are likely wondering how you're supposed to go about it. There are many strategies for investing, so it is important that you choose the one that works for you. Before we begin diving too deep into the strategies themselves, let's take some time to explore what you need to know so that you can discover which strategy is the best for you. This chapter will help you set your goals clearly and assist you in exploring the options available to you based on those goals.

How to Choose the Strategy That You Need

Choosing the strategy that you need to get the most out of your investments starts with understanding what you actually want to get out of them. Once you are clear on what your goals are, you can begin to understand what types of investment strategies might fit in with your goals. Each investment strategy has a unique opportunity, outcome, and financial requirement. Knowing that the one you picked should perfectly fit several of your own unique needs and requirements can help successfully fulfill your goals.

The following sections will help you set clear goals, understand how much work you are willing to put into your investments, recognizing the benefits of unique investment types, and understanding where you should start. Know that this may seem a little bit overwhelming at first, but it is actually quite simple. Once you understand what you are doing and where you want to start, it becomes a lot easier. We will also discuss your portfolio in the next chapter so that you can get a better understanding of how to create a long-term plan, in addition to an idea of where you should start.

Know What You Desire to Get Out of Your Investments

Understanding what you want to get out of your investments is important. This is essentially where you get to build your investment goals. Here, you get the opportunity to decide what it is that you are most focused on when it comes to your investments. You can also discover your secondary goals, and any other goals you may have. In general, there are four goals that exist when people make investments: short-term growth, long-term growth, residual income, and personal financial asset protection. We will explore each of these goals so that you can understand what they are and why they're relevant. In general, most people have at least 2 or 3, if not all of these goals with their funds. Right now, we want to focus on your primary goals. Once you have discovered those, you can begin making your earliest moves to support your primary goals. Then, as you diversify your portfolio you can begin to focus on your secondary goals.

Short-Term Growth

When your goals are focused on the short-term, this typically means that you have something that you want or need to use the funds for within a year or less. In some cases, it can be as long as 18 months. However, the standard time for short-term investments is about 12 months in length, if not less. Using short-term investment strategies means that you can easily access your funds after that short period of time for whatever you desire to use it for. For example, if you know you want to go on a major trip next summer, want to buy a new car, or do anything else that requires a significant chunk of money but can be completed in a shorter time frame, using short-term investments is the best way to go.

Many people, if not all, have some type of short-term investment strategy in place. This strategy requires a little more time and commitment, as you do have to regularly go in and revisit your strategy and reinforce it after it has reached fruition. However, this is not typically a big deal.

The best way to determine if your goal classifies as a short-term goal is to ask yourself: "Will I need these funds in 12 months or less?" If you will, you know that your primary goal is to have access to your funds soon, meaning that you want to have a short-term investment strategy in place. Doing this may seem ineffective, but the reality is that it is highly beneficial. Using short-term investment strategies means that you can protect your funds against inflation while you save them up. This is more effective than merely keeping the funds in a savings account.

Long-Term Growth

Long-term growth goals are ones that are typically effective after a period of 2 years or longer. The average term ranges from 5-10 years, or above 25 years. You often see people using long-term growth solutions to help them save for retirement or for other far-off life experiences. These funds are also great for anyone who may not have any particular goal with their funds but know that they do want to keep them in a protected space. This means that their future-funds can be protected against inflation better than if they were simply stored in a standard savings account.

Long-term growth tends to be the second primary goal for many people. In general, most people want some form of short-term financial investment that they can use quickly, and some form of long-term investment that they can use to protect their future selves against inflation, as well as to save for future events. This may include things such as college for their children as well. The long-term savings are not always intended solely for the individual, as sometimes it is used for future generations instead.

The best way to determine if a long-term investment strategy is the best for you is to ask yourself: "Will I need these funds in the next 2 years?" If not, you can likely put them straight into a long-term investment fund. This will ensure that they are stashed away, protected against inflation, and working for you.

Residual Income

If your goal is to increase your earning potential and maximize your monthly and annual profits, you want an investment strategy that has a residual income benefit. Technically, any investment strategy that increases the funds you have available to you through profits can be considered residual income. For the purpose of this goal, we are talking about an investment that can be maintained while it provides you with regular profits in the meantime.

The best way to open yourself up to this type of residual income is to begin investing in things such as real estate. When you invest in real estate, in particular, your profits are immediate as well as long-term, depending on how much you invest. In order to create this duality in your investment, you want to purchase a piece of real estate where you would receive income through monthly rental fees. This means that you will be receiving continuous payments from your investment, in addition to having the value of the property itself reserved as a long-term investment.

Personal Financial Asset Protection

Many people do not realize that having insurance is also a form of investment. Although you do not necessarily stand to gain money from insurance, having it in place does protect you against potential losses. As such, it can be considered an investment. In addition to having insurance, another way that you can protect your financial assets is to diversify your portfolio. As you will learn shortly, this is not something you should do right away. Instead, you should aim to focus on one area and then grow from there. However, if you know this is a primary goal for you, then growth would be something that you should focus on incorporating into your strategy early, rather than waiting longer like some other investors tend to do.

Defining Your Goals

The best way to make sure that you are clear on your goals is to look deeply and understand exactly what your goals are. Sit honestly with yourself and explore what it is that you desire to achieve from your investments. Then, you can easily begin to discover what matters most to you. If you feel that you are drawn toward all four main goals, or that you have additional ones that have not been listed, pay attention to ordering them in terms of priority.

Once you have discovered what your goals are and what your priorities are, you will have a better idea of where to start and what to focus on when it comes to investing. This will ensure that any move you make is directly in alignment with your goal, rather than pursuing it because someone else told you it was a good idea. Remember, at the end of the day the funds being invested are yours and you get the final say on what is right for you. The best way you can confidently make that decision is to educate yourself on the facts that go into it, just like you are doing right now!

Be Realistic About How Much Work You Are Willing to Do

Now that you understand what your goals are, you can begin to discover what you are willing to do to actually make them happen. For example, if your goal is to create residual income, but you do not want to be directly involved in the rental market, you might consider that this would be a goal for the future, and maybe not necessarily a primary goal. Alternatively, if you have the funds available to you, you may instead choose to get involved and hire a management team to take over. While this would cut into your profitability, it would also reduce the amount of work required from you when it comes to your investments.

Based on the above scenario, it is clear that you need to understand how much time you are willing to invest into your financial goals, and how much funds you have available to you if the time you need to invest is not worthwhile for you or possible for you at this moment. If the time you have to invest seems too much, you should consider starting with a different goal. For example, investing in mutual funds or the stock market.

Once you are clear on the amount of time you have to invest, you have to make sure that you do not waste any investments by getting involved in something that you do not actually have the time to see through. Fortunately, most investment opportunities are fairly easy to deal with in terms of time. Most do not require you to invest too much time. The least-involved investment strategies include you hiring a portfolio manager and meeting with your manager once per quarter to ensure that your goals are being met and that you update any information as you see fit. So, understand that even if you don't have a large amount of time to invest in your investing strategies, you do still have many offers available to you.

Understanding the Minimum Entry Requirements

In addition to investing time, you also need to think of how much money you can invest. Every strategy you look at will have a minimum entry requirement for you before you can get started. While investing is no longer reserved for those who are particularly wealthy, you still need to have a sufficient amount of funds to start out with. Assess what you have available to you immediately and make your earliest decisions based on that. Once you begin to grow your funds, you can then begin to diversify your portfolio and include those more costly investments that have a higher buy-in value.

Picking Your Starting Point

Now that you are clear on what your goal is, the time required by different investments, and the number of funds you have available to get started with, you should have a fairly clear idea of what your 'launch point' or starting point is for investing. If you have looked over these three things and realize they don't match up, for example, you don't have much time or funds to invest, but you want to get started in real estate or something similar that will offer residual income, ideally you should be choosing a secondary goal that is more accessible to you at the moment. Then, once you reach that goal you can use the funds to go ahead and get started in real estate.

It is important that these three values: your goal, your time, and your startup funds, are in alignment. If for whatever reason they are not, there's a chance your investments might fail. This is because at least one aspect will be out of place and therefore your investment may simply not be affordable, may not work out, or maybe too much for you to effectively handle. For this reason, make sure you start somewhere that is tangible and manageable for you at the moment. Understand that the entire point of getting started in investing is for you to increase your funds, so you can always go ahead and move toward your other primary or secondary goals later on once they become more feasible with your financial standing.

A Note on Starting Out: Choose One to Start

Before we move on, I want to point out one very important thing: when you choose a starting point, choose only one. Too many people make the mistake of going into an investor's office or otherwise and expecting to start out with several different investment funds all at the same time. Unfortunately, many investors will actually agree with this and go ahead with it because they want to offer you the service you are looking for, and they typically make money from it. For you, however, this can be overwhelming and can result in you not getting your needs met.

If you are just starting out, chances are you have not yet found an investor to work with that can understand your needs, works in the way that best suits you, and complements your personality. If you are not working with an investor but instead are going solo, this becomes even more important.

When you are starting out, only start with a single strategy. Just one type of investment. Doing this will ensure that you master that style before moving forward. The same goes for if you are going to an investor. Make sure that you take some time to understand the important concepts, get into the swing of things, understand your investor, and make sure that the entire process runs smoothly before adding anything else to the portfolio. Investing, when done properly, runs like a well-oiled machine. There is no need to waste your time jumping in feet first, getting confused, and potentially making fatal mistakes that deter you from achieving success. Instead, start small with a single focus and grow out from there, one at a time.

Chapter 3: Understanding Your Investment Portfolio

Now that you know your goals and desires, it is time for you to understand your investment portfolio! In this chapter, we are going to cover the basics of your portfolio. This will help ensure that you know what a portfolio is, why it matters, what it looks like, what your goals with your portfolio are, and how you will manage your portfolio.

Your Portfolio Accounts for All of Your Investments

Put simply, your portfolio is the sum of all of your current investments. Whenever you invest in something, it goes into your portfolio. If created properly, your portfolio should clearly reflect your investment goals. For example, if your goal is primarily focused on long-term growth, all of the items within your portfolio should easily identify that and prove it through the investments that are stored within it.

Each time you add a new form of investment to your account, you are adding it to your portfolio. Your portfolio takes the sum of everything and shows yourself, as well as investors, what you are doing with your money and what your focuses are. You can easily look into your portfolio and see if you are successfully and efficiently managing your funds, or if they are not being invested in your best interests. Early on, you may find that it is difficult for you to successfully do it all on your own. This is why it is beneficial to start with just one single investment type in the beginning and move out one at a time. You may find that an investor can help you easily ensure that your portfolio is being managed in the most effective way possible, thus ensuring that you are getting the most out of your funds in a way that easily fuels your goals, rather than hinders your ability to reach them.

What It Means to Diversify Your Portfolio

Diversifying your portfolio essentially means that you are adding new strategies to it. For example, if you started out with something simple like mutual funds and then decided that you wanted to invest in stocks, you are already diversifying your portfolio.

There are two ways that your portfolio can be diversified: investing in new accounts with the same strategy (for example, investing in different types of mutual fund, purchasing real estate in a different city or country, etc.) or, by investing in a new strategy entirely. Typically, you want to start by diversifying within a single strategy before you move on to adding a new one altogether. However, that also depends entirely on what your goals are.

When it comes to the stock market, diversifying is unique. Let's focus on this for a moment so that, should you choose to include the stocks in your portfolio, you will understand what diversifying them means. Essentially, diversifying means investing in many different businesses or commodities so that if one falls or crashes, you are hedged by the others. In every case, you are still invested in the stocks. However, by diversifying who and what you have invested in, you have made it easier for yourself to maximize your income and minimize your risk.

Should You Manage Your Own Portfolio?

Ideally, you should be directly involved in managing your own portfolio. However, you may choose to include an investor in the management as well if you want to make it efficient and less time-consuming. Additionally, including a professional investor means that you are less at-risk of having your investments fall flat or result in you taking a loss of some form. Since investors are highly trained in investing and have a clearer idea of how they can maximize your income and minimize your risk, having a professional on-board is typically a great idea.

It is important to understand, still, what different investment types are and what they mean, however. You want to make sure that if you do choose to hire an investor, you choose one who is acting in your best interest. The best way to make sure of this is to arm yourself with knowledge so that you have a greater understanding of what your investor is talking about, what they are offering you, what they are doing with your funds, and what they should be doing. This is how you can ensure that their actions will benefit you and will focus on the goals you have in mind.

Chapter 4: Banking on Inflation

Banking on inflation essentially means that you are banking on a commodity that is known to match market inflation effortlessly. While this is true for virtually all investment styles, those classified in this specific category tend to be ones that are easier for you to invest in on your own, without the help of an investor or a banker's assistance. In this chapter, you are going to learn about how you can bank on inflation yourself, through three primary strategies.

Types of Strategies that Bank on Inflation

There are three primary strategies that allow you to bank on inflation on your own, without requiring the assistance of an investor or a banker directly overseeing your investments for you. They include real estate, precious goods, and currency. When you choose to invest in these three strategies with the intention of banking on inflation, your goal is to essentially buy low and sell high. In many cases, you will end up holding on to the commodity for years before you end up selling it. This means that it has typically endured a high amount of inflation and has given you the opportunity to maximize your gains.

If you are someone who has the desire to use investments so you can pass on your wealth to future generations in your family, then you may be particularly inspired to invest in this field. Things such as real estate and precious goods can easily be passed down to future generations so that they can then overlook the investment and, if they see fit, sell it to maximize their profits as well. Let's begin exploring each individual investment option and why they are such a benefit to you as an investor!

Real Estate

Real estate is a great all-around investment for those who can afford it. When you invest in real estate, it provides you the opportunity to create residual income, in addition to long-term growth. Real estate does have a high buy-in value, but there are some ways that you can overcome this. For example, purchasing real estate with a partner or a group of people as opposed to doing it alone. This would allow you to buy a share of the property, rather than buying it outright yourself. If you would prefer to own real estate personally, doing this can initially allow you to raise the capital to go ahead and do it yourself in the future.

When you invest in real estate, you hedge yourself against many different types of financial risks. For example, inflation. When you purchase real estate when the market is low (or in a state that is regularly called a 'buyer's market') you provide yourself with the perfect opportunity to gain possession over something that can earn you an incredible profit. Whether you choose to immediately sell it once the market swings back in the other direction, or hold on to it for many years and earn rental income from it, you can make a great deal of money through real estate.

You should know that there are two ways that real estate can become an investment: through flipping properties, or through buying and renting real estate. When you 'flip' properties, you essentially purchase old run down properties, rebuild or renovate the property, and then sell it as fast as you can. Typically, the shorter amount of time that the house is in your possession, the better. Alternatively, if you are buying a house to rent it out, you want to keep it in your possession for as long as possible. It then becomes an investment in two ways: through residual income, and through long-term growth profits.

In both cases, you do not necessarily have to be heavily involved in the process if you do not want to be. You can easily hire a team to overlook the work and ensure that you stay hands-off as much as possible. Then, your only involvement would be to locate homes, purchase them at exactly the right time, and then turn them over to your team. They would then become responsible for overseeing all of the work done to ensure that it is either flipped in a short period of time or maintained over a long period of time with renters in the house at all times.

Although hiring a team does cut into your profitability, it also gives you plenty of freedom since you have someone to delegate most of the tasks to. If, however, this does not matter to you, then you can certainly be more hands-on. For example, being directly involved in the flipping process, or being directly involved with your renters and overseeing the landlord duties that are required to maintain your property.

A 'final property management' circumstance arises when you are investing in a group. In this situation, the group usually decides on what to do and will often hire a management team to overlook the day-to-day needs of handling the property. At this point, your job is only to cut a check for the group and have the manager overlooking the entire investment keep you updated on the property.

Real estate truly is an incredible investment opportunity for many reasons. If you have the amount of time required to invest in it, as well as the finances available, getting started in real estate can be highly profitable. It offers many of the benefits that investors are looking for, and does not necessarily have to come at a high time-cost.

Precious Goods

One interesting way to invest is to purchase precious goods. Precious metals and other highly valuable items, such as vintage cars that have been maintained incredibly well, can actually be a wonderful investment. Not only are they typically cherished by their owner, but they also tend to hold a high value and can resell at an incredible price for the owner if they should ever desire to sell it.

The best way to make a profit through precious goods is to look for opportunities to purchase them at a lower price and then hold onto them while their value increases. With this tactic, the value increases over time. This means that you should only invest in precious goods if you intend on staying invested in them for a long-term growth opportunity. This is not a valuable short-term growth strategy. It may also be too risky for those who are planning to bank on them as their retirement fund, so be sure to have this as a secondary option if you truly want to invest but rely on the funds involved!

It is ideal to invest in these goods by using your extra money. For example, creating a secondary retirement investment strategy before proceeding. This would create the potential to significantly increase your profits so that you have even more when you are ready to retire. However, there's also the possibility that their value might fall and not earn you the profit you were hoping for.

The best way to invest in these goods is to find them on a sale or at auctions. However, if you are purchasing precious metals, you can also purchase them directly from dealers. Again, you want to purchase them in any situation where you can get them for the lowest price possible to maximize your overall profits.

Currency

Many people choose to invest in currency as an opportunity to hedge against inflation. An easy way to explain is this, imagine you purchased $1000 USD back when the United States Dollar was not performing as strongly as the Canadian Dollar. Then, when the United States Dollar swung back up in value and became stronger than the Canadian Dollar, you went ahead and purchased Canadian Dollars. If you continued doing this, your funds would significantly increase. This means that you would maximize your profitability simply by investing in currency.

You can easily do this yourself, or you can do it with the help of an investor. Alternatively, investing in currency is also something that you can do directly in the stock market. If you want to get involved with the stock market, you can get involved with currencies right there.

Currency investments are a great way to maximize your profits, but it takes quite some time to do it. They should not be relied on as a solitary or primary investment strategy. Instead, they should be a supplementary or additional strategy. Since sometimes it can take even longer than a decade, for the currency to swing back in the alternative direction, and it is certainly something that requires plenty of patience.

Chapter 5: Types of Investment Funds

The following types of investments are investment funds that you can get involved in. These are low maintenance and are wonderful for anyone looking for either short-term or long-term investment solutions. Each one has a unique set of benefits to it, though most of them generally work the same way. You provide money and someone else overlooks the rest. All you truly have to do is meet with your advisor on a scheduled basis, typically every 3-6 months, to ensure that your investments are still performing optimally and that your relevant goals are being met. In this chapter, we will have a look at these investment funds and what they mean for you.

Mutual Funds

Mutual funds are a type of fund that involves shareholders (you) investing their funds in a 'mutual' fund. That is where the name come from. The fund is then watched over by a professional management team and is typically traded in some way or another. These trades may involve real estate, the stock market, or other investment strategies. Then, when you are ready, you can draw on the fund.

It is important that you pay attention to what the terms of the funds are. While they don't tend to be a fixed-term investment, some do prefer that you keep your investments with the fund for a longer period of time. As such, they may require you to sign an agreement to do so. If you decide that you want to draw on your funds sooner, there is usually a high fee that you will have to pay. It is important to understand how much that fee is and to be as certain as you possibly can that those funds are easily capable of staying there long-term. While an unexpected situation may arise, the goal is not to need the funds until you've reached the maturity date.

You can easily get involved in mutual funds through an investor. Investment advisors are the easiest way to do so, as they are typically directly involved with the professional management team that is responsible for overlooking the funds. You can get in touch with one of these advisors independently, or through a bank. They tend to operate in a variety of financial institutions, so they are fairly easy to come by. Ideally, however, you want to pick an advisor who you can rely on for many things, so make sure that you like them!

Bonds

Bonds are like a loan that you give to the bank. They are a form of debt that the bank creates with you. As such, they work virtually the same as a loan would for you, only in the opposite direction. Instead of you borrowing money from the bank and paying them an interest fee, the bank borrows money from you and pays you an interest fee.

The money will either be loaned directly to the bank, or may be loaned to the government, a city, a company, or anyone else. Essentially, the entity will borrow the money and promise to pay you back, with regular interest payments involved. This is a very safe investment strategy for anyone who is planning to get involved with investments but wants to protect themselves against the many risks that tend to arise from making an investment.

While bonds can be made available directly, the easiest way to get involved with this particular type of investment is through your advisor once again. Your advisor will make the appropriate arrangements with your funds to get them into the bond and get your profits back in the future if necessary. Additionally, working together with an advisor and financial institution ensures that the entity borrowing the money has been checked. You want to make sure that they are genuine, or that they can actually pay back the promised funds. If you are doing this privately or independently, it is necessary that you also take the appropriate steps to ensure that your loan will be paid in full and that the person or entity that you are loaning it to will not default on the loan. Doing it privately can earn you a higher percentage, but it can also put you at a higher risk. It is completely your choice whether or not you are willing to take that risk, though it is not usually advised unless you can be absolutely sure that the entity will pay you back.

Bank Products

There are many bank products available to you that make it easy to increase your funds through investments. Many of these products rely on the basic structure of a mutual fund or a bond, though they are specialized to meet the needs of specific goals. The most common ones include short-term and long-term savings with no specific needs, as well as retirements savings, education savings, and other types of specific savings.

The benefit of going to a bank is that your entire account is overlooked by the bank and that you are not required to do much to keep it going. If you do it through your own bank, it can also be easy to access and watch over as it grows, as in many cases these will be visible directly from your online banking application.

However, investing in these funds is considered somewhat conservative. This means that you won't make as much money through banking products as you will through other services and products. Although they are still a valuable tool, they may be insufficient for some investors. If you are someone who wants to take more risks to make more profits, you might want to stay away from these options or keep them as secondary choices. If you are someone who prefers conservative risk, then this may be the perfect solution for you!

In order to discover exactly what solutions are available to you, the best thing you can do is to go to your bank. Often, they will sit down with you and discuss your goals and provide you with the solutions that best meet the needs of your goals. As previously mentioned, these solutions are tailored to the specifics such as education or retirement savings, meaning that they are specifically designed to benefit those goals and, therefore, everything is geared towards helping you reach them.

Insurance

Another type of investment you can invest in is insurance. While insurance will not increase your profits, it is considered an investment as it does protect you and your assets. There are many different types of insurance that you can consider depending on what your needs are. Below are a few of the basics that you should know about:

Life insurance

Life insurance is a form of insurance that protects your family. Should you pass away, your life insurance would be made available to your beneficiary or beneficiaries. This could then be used to pay off your mortgage, any outstanding debt you may have, your funeral, and anything else that may need to be paid off. Anything remaining would then be a small lump sum made available to your family for whatever they may want or need to do with it.

Life insurance is beneficial if you tend to carry around a lot of debt, don't have a large amount of savings put away for your family should you pass away, or want to otherwise ensure that your family does not have to carry your financial burdens should you pass away.

Critical Illness Insurance

Critical illness insurance is a form of insurance that is made available to you should you ever fall critically ill. This insurance typically pays out in the instance that you are too ill to work or do anything. Essentially, the funds are intended to be used to cover your monthly expenses as well as your medical expenses. This can be valuable if you want to make sure that both you and your family do not have to carry your financial burdens should you ever be afflicted by a terrible health condition.

Unemployment Insurance

If you ever become unemployed, unemployment insurance is necessary. Most employers automatically pay this for you. Self-employed individuals are required to pay this themselves. Unemployment insurance becomes available to you if you ever lose your job. This ensures that you can cover the cost of living until you can get a new job. It is valuable as you have something to fall back on should anything happen to your job.

Homeowners Insurance

Homeowners insurance is available to homeowners to ensure that if anything were to ever happen to their home, they would be protected. For example, if their home was burned down or robbed, their losses would be covered by the insurance company. This is essentially a sweeping asset insurance, as it covers your home and everything inside of it. Another form of home insurance exists for tenants, known as 'tenant's insurance.' This does not directly provide the property with insurance but instead insures the tenant. Then, should anything ever happen, the tenant is covered. For example, if their unit was the first to catch on fire in an apartment building, their insurance would cover them. Or, if their home was robbed, their items would be repurchased by the insurance company.

Other Types of Insurance

There are many other types of insurances that exist out there. Just to name a few, there are other kinds like car insurance or precious asset insurance which are both used to protect expensive assets that you own. Debt insurance is purchased to protect your debt should you default. For example, if you lost your job then your debt insurance would cover your minimum payment for a set period of time. There is also pet insurance, health insurance, dental insurance, and more.

Chapter 6: Understanding Stocks

Stocks are another really incredible investment opportunity for people to get involved in. If you want to get started on investing in the stock market, you can either do so directly or through an investment agency. If you do it directly, you will need to download the software required. Ideally, then, you would want to purchase a guidebook directly on that software so that you can maximize your earning potential. The stock market has a lot of ins and outs for people to learn about should they want to make a profit out of it. There is simply too much for me to cover in this book. However, if you are interested in the stock market and want to understand it better, then use the assistance of a broker and an account manager to oversee your stock market involvement, this chapter is for you!

The Stock Market, Is It for You?

The stock market is a highly volatile trading platform. Although it can make you a lot of money, it can cause you to lose a lot too. It is important that if you get involved in stocks that you refrain from investing any funds that are necessary or important to you. Instead, invest your extra funds. In doing so, you eliminate any unnecessary risks that can harm you, and won't have so much 'riding on' the investment.

Although the stock market is volatile, it has the potential to earn you an incredible amount of money. Many people have become millionaires thanks to the stock market, simply because they have learned how to use it effectively. If you are looking for the opportunity to earn an incredible profit, the stock market is a great place to start. You can either learn how to do it yourself and invest your own time in earning profits, or you can hire someone else. If you intend on doing it yourself, know that you are going to have to invest quite a bit of time to make sure you'll make a profit. Stocks are something that has to be watched regularly so you don't end up taking a major hit. If you decide to hire someone else, the next section will give you some information on how you can do that and what to look for.

Brokers and Account Managers

Brokers are the people responsible for helping others find their way in the stock market. They may be large, or small. Account managers are the individuals who work for the brokers and they're the ones who work with you directly. These two work together to ensure that once you are prepared, you won't have problems making your way through the stock market. In essence, all you have to do is find a reliable broker and account manager and set up an appointment with them. Assuming that you like their style, that they have impressed you, and that you feel confident with picking them, you can then agree to allow them to oversee your account and you can let them take over your stock management.

Ideally, there are a few things you should look out for to ensure that the assistance you're being given is actually helpful. First off, arming yourself with as much knowledge about the stock market as you can is important. Understand that when you invest in the stock market you can try the lower risk categories, however, there is no such thing as investments with no risk. If someone tells you otherwise, this could be a sign that they're not being completely honest with you. Do not believe them even if they say that there is virtually no risk. This alludes to the idea that you do not have to worry. While you do not necessarily have to keep on worrying, you should know that the stocks are volatile, and your advisor should be open and honest with you about this. However, they should also assert that their company has a lot of experience with handling stocks and that they know how to effectively manage your account to minimize your risk. That is a safe and positive word to hear from an advisor.

You also want to make sure that the advisor is professional, and that they understand your needs. If they do not seem like they have the time to hear you out, or if they do not understand your wants, even after you have explained it to them, then they may be working for their own interests instead of yours. While they are being paid for their job to manage your account, you want to make sure that they are managing your account in a way that guarantees you'll be the one who benefits in the end. That is how they stay in business. If they are managing your account for their own selfish purposes, you should not invest in them.

Lastly, in the appointment, you want to make sure that it is you who will set the expectations. Not only should your goals be clearly laid out, but you should also ensure that you and your advisor are both on the same page about how the investments will be made, and how all follow-ups will be done. In other words, you should have a clear idea as to when you will meet again to discuss growth and progress.

How Money Is Made

In the stock market, money is made specifically by buying low and selling high. However, there are a few different ways in which this is done. For those who are involved in incredibly fast stock markets, they typically get involved in what is called 'scalping.' This essentially means buying a large number of stocks and selling them as soon as they've gone up a few cents in value. As a result, they earn a few dollars at a time. The idea here is to buy a massive amount of stocks while you wait for a small amount of growth. This is incredibly time-consuming, but it does earn a fairly decent profit for those who use it.

The next type is called 'day trading.' These are usually the trades that opens when the stock market opens and closes when it closes. These trades are shorter in length but do not require a rapid response like scalping the market. A trade may take minutes or hours, but will always be closed by the end of the day.

The last type of stock market trading requires you to wait quite some time. In general, you invest in an account or stock that is considered to be conservative and you let your funds sit for a long period of time. Then, when you are ready to take your profits, you simply go ahead and sell the next time the market is on the uptrend. These types of investments are typically made in massive corporations or in currencies that are known to be on the general uptrend. Since the stock market itself is always on the uptrend, if you get involved with stocks that are less risky, you know that they will be easier for you to get involved in and stay in for a long period of time. A common situation where we see this is with cryptocurrencies, which we will discuss next.

A Note on Cryptocurrencies

Cryptocurrencies are traded like stocks in the stock market. They are, however, traded on their own market. That is unless you are investing in the company and not the currency. For example, if you invest in Bitcoin the company, you would invest in the regular stock market. But if you invested in Bitcoins the currency, you would invest in the special cryptocurrency market. Both have been known to be highly valuable ways of increasing your funds, and remain extremely popular in the modern market. Much like with trading your own stocks in general, however, there is far more to explain that can reasonably fit within this guide. So, it is important that you understand that if you want to get involved directly with the currencies themselves as opposed to the companies that own the currencies, you need to have a look at cryptocurrency-specific trading guides that can help you get started so you can earn high profits.

Conclusion

Thank you for reading *Investing for Beginners: The Only Money Guide You'll Ever Need.*

This guide was designed to arm you with the best knowledge and understanding the countless possibilities when it comes to investing. Investing is an incredibly powerful solution for maximizing your savings and increasing your earning potential. While it was once reserved for the elite and wealthy, it is now an incredibly necessary strategy for anyone who desires to have money long-term.

I hope that this book was able to equip you with enough knowledge so you can feel confident in investing your money. Knowing how valuable and important it is to invest, it is equally important that you feel confident in the act of investing itself. Knowing as much as you can about investing and different strategies will give you the wisdom to make the best decisions with your funds so you won't ever feel like you made an unwise decision based on a lack of education around the choice.

The next step is to take action on the goals you have defined for yourself. You can either do so directly or take the necessary action of hiring a financial advisor who can overlook your account and help you. Remember, even if you hire an advisor you still need to keep up to speed with the knowledge and the current state of financial affairs. The more knowledge you have, the better you can advocate for yourself in your advisor-to-client relationship and ensure that your exact needs and desires are being met.

Lastly, if you enjoyed *Investing for Beginners: The Only Money Guide You'll Ever Need*. I ask that you please take the time to review it. Your honest feedback would be greatly appreciated.

Thank you!

Did you know that a large percent of people who make a lot of money lose it within the first couple years?

It doesn't take much for a person to lose all of their money. Around 2 in 3 lottery winners lose all of their winnings within 5 years. If someone could lose hundreds of millions of dollars over a couple years, how fast will you lose your millions that you could make from this book?

Over the past couple years I have stumbled upon the key secret behind managing money and KEEPING it. If you follow the link below you will uncover the truth behind managing and keeping the money you make

>>> Click/Tap here to Learn the Secret Behind Money Management <<<

Or Go to https://secretstomoneymanagement.gr8.com/

Description

Investing for Beginners: The Only Money Guide You'll Ever Need is a powerful investment guide that was designed to help beginners get started in investing.

It is important to understand that investing is no longer a strategy that is reserved for the elite and wealthy. Instead, it is a smart and necessary strategy for anyone who desires to have any form of financial stability in their life.

Effectively investing your funds will help meet both your short-term and long-term goals with ease. Proper investments make sure that your money is always working for you and that you are not exposed to the ever-rising threat of inflation.

If you are new to the world of investing, *Investing for Beginners: The Only Money Guide You'll Ever Need* is a descriptive guide that will ensure that you are equipped with all of the knowledge you need to start out strong. As long as you are armed with valuable knowledge and understanding, you can be certain that you will become a strong investor and that you will surely reach your financial goals.

Just because anyone can get started on investing doesn't mean that just about anyone should do it. The only people who should truly get involved are those who are willing to educate themselves and maximize their profitability through knowledge and understanding. You can start now by reading, *Investing for Beginners: The Only Money Guide You'll Ever Need*. By the end, you will feel empowered to make smart choices with your investments so that you can become a powerful investor, too!

www.ingramcontent.com/pod-product-compliance
Lightning Source LLC
Chambersburg PA
CBHW070512220526
45467CB00002B/631